SUPERVISOR

SELECTION, T

AND DEVELO

SUPERVISORS: THEIR SELECTION, TRAINING AND DEVELOPMENT

by Trevor Foxen and Trevor Peck

Revised by Bob Dixon

The Industrial Society

First published 1976 by
The Industrial Society
Peter Runge House
3 Carlton House Terrace
London SW1Y 5DG
Telephone: 01-839 4300

Fourth edition 1989
© *The Industrial Society, 1976, 1980, 1983, 1989*

ISBN 0 85290 433 9

British Library Cataloguing in Publication Data

Foxen, Trevor
    Supervisors.
    1. Supervisors. Training
    I. Title   II. Peck, Trevor   III. Dixon, Bob
    IV. Series
    658.4'071245

Typeset by Ace Filmsetting Ltd, Frome, Somerset
Printed and bound in Great Britain by Belmont Press, Northampton

CONTENTS

Foreword   vi

I   **Supervisors: Their Selection, Training**   **1**
     and Development
   1   What is a Supervisor?
   2   The Purpose of a Supervisor
   3   Selecting Your Supervisors
   4   Preparing for Supervision
   5   Training Your Supervisors
   6   The Supervisor as a Leader
   7   Communication
   8   Developing and Maintaining Progress

II   **Appendices**   **31**
   1   The supervisor as a professional manager
   2   Supervising people at work
   3   Example job description for a
      typical supervisor
   4   Professional bodies and qualifications
   5   Example selection and induction training
      from a large national company

Further Reading   **44**

FOREWORD

Whatever the discipline or level of management, the responsibilities of a manager are many and various. It is their job to produce results with essentially just two resources—people and time.

To maximise the potential of both, most managers need some reminders and basic guidelines to help them.

The Notes for Managers series provides succinct yet comprehensive coverage of key management issues and skills. The short time it takes to read each title will pay dividends in terms of utilising one of those key resources—people.

ALISTAIR GRAHAM
Director, The Industrial Society

I

SUPERVISORS: THEIR
SELECTION, TRAINING
AND DEVELOPMENT

1

WHAT IS A SUPERVISOR?

Before talking about supervisors or supervisory training, or indeed their selection, it is important to understand what we mean by the term supervisor.

Strictly speaking, a supervisor is anyone in charge of others; those with whom he or she is required to carry out the objectives of the operation, whether production or service. This definition could, of course, include, in the broadest sense, the directors of most organisations, for it covers anyone in charge of others who has objectives to meet.

Not unnaturally, many of the items discussed in this booklet will apply equally to all levels of management. However, the primary target is those members of first line management most often directly related to the workforce at the point of production or service.

Supervisors can come in many guises, varying from leading hand, through chargehand, foreman, administrative officer, head of department, team leader, or indeed manager. They remain, however, the first line of management, and to the workforce they are 'the management'. They are, after all, the leaders of the work-group. Few levels of management have greater opportunity to influence the workforce or contribute at the final level of activity.

Often, they are loaded with responsibility yet devoid of the authority or trust to achieve reasonable objectives. Supervisors have described themselves varyingly as 'the forgotten legion', 'a necessary evil', 'bosses' buffers' or 'the meat in the organisation sandwich'—to quote but a few.

It is hoped that, after reading this booklet, a better understanding of the selection, training and use of supervisors will result.

2

THE PURPOSE OF
A SUPERVISOR

Supervisors (first line managers) exist to meet the needs of current practice in workplace structure.

People involved in any activity require a common point of reference if they are not to lose direction in seeking to achieve their objectives. This common point is the work-group leader, i.e. supervisor/manager. There are numerous examples, even in primitive societies, where this is so. When people are left to their own devices a leader *will* emerge, but will not necessarily lead people towards the aims and objectives of the organisation. Perhaps the following statement would sum it up in a way that would not provoke universal disagreement, always accepting there are almost as many definitions of the purpose of a supervisor as there are supervisors.

'To be responsible for the smooth running and production of the goods or services under their control through the resources available to them.'

Of those resources, perhaps the most crucial, demanding, frustrating, challenging and rewarding are people. To many people their supervisor is the company. Supervisors are involved to a lesser or greater degree in the following functions: planning, costing, delegation, evaluation, organising, cost control, interviewing, selection, industrial relations, discipline, setting targets, counselling, standards, appraisal, training, human relations, communication and co-ordination, among others.

Many, looking at the above functions, will quite naturally

3

observe that these are the areas that managers operate in. It implies that supervisors *are* managers. Unfortunately this is often not recognised by their own managers, colleagues, subordinates and, more significantly, by the supervisors themselves! The reasons for this are many and varied.

Before the advent of greater organisation of work people at shop-floor level by the trade unions, supervisors were the focal point of all the pressures resulting from changes of company policy and market requirements.

This greater organisation through the unions brought about an improvement not only in working conditions and wages, but also increased union influence in those areas previously considered as the supervisors' 'territory'. This resulted in supervisors becoming the 'whipping boys'. The people below, above and at the same level rarely showed any respect. In short, these managers became the lost 'men in the middle'. This resulted in the role and purpose of supervisors becoming blurred almost to the extent of appearing not to be there.

The importance of the supervisor cannot be too highly emphasised. This is particularly true when today's need for greater commitment on the part of people at their work is taken into account. Just as poor or misguided supervision can be costly in terms of disputes, turnover, absence etc., it follows that good, well trained, well led supervision is the most effective.

If managing directors are supervisors of their directors, it is logical that supervisors are managers of their teams and an integral part of the management structure. The purpose of supervisors will be more effectively fulfilled if they are well selected, prepared, trained and developed and their role clearly defined.

3

SELECTING YOUR
SUPERVISORS

Few people would claim to have found a foolproof method of selection; there are, however, some basic rules that could be constructively followed when selecting supervisors. Most well structured organisations should be in a position to 'grow their own'. This system has the added advantages of knowing what you are getting and motivating the better employees by making opportunities available.

If honest standards of performance and appraisal exist, there should be information available to indicate a large fund of people with supervisory potential. This, added to pre- and post-promotion training (*see* Appendix 5), should make the home-grown supervisor a very capable person indeed.

Selecting supervisory staff

A prospective supervisor must:

● honestly want to do the job
● have some record of success
● have the ability to grow
● be ultimately acceptable to any work-group (fit in)
● receive basic management training *before* being appointed
● know exactly what is expected and have *agreed* objectives
● help plan his or her own induction programme and know who will help carry this out
● be given the authority and trust needed to function properly.

Do not be misled into thinking no one is yet ready for promotion—often, only the opportunity is needed to discover your 'star supervisor'. Too much delay can result in the loss of individuals or their talents and will to perform.

Supervisors should not be selected on the 'first available' principle, nor by default. Often, talent can be spotted by observing 'stand-ins' or 'substitutes' during holidays or other short periods. It should never be assumed that the 'best' fitter–secretary–clerk will necessarily make the best supervisor.

In the past, some organisations appear to have followed the rule of appointing shop stewards to supervisory positions. There is no reason in the world why a shop steward should not make a good supervisor—they are, after all, employees as well as shop stewards, and have equal status in the selection stakes. What is sometimes in dispute is the reasoning behind such selection. The very worst reason is to move a bothersome steward; the best reason is selecting a steward who has shown the vital signs of leadership and organising ability together with the ability to communicate effectively. It is wrong if a shop steward is not considered for promotion because of union activities. All employees should have equal opportunity, and selection must be made in the most objective way possible.

Important factors to consider are those of showing leadership ability and being acceptable to the work-group. Leadership ability may be ascertained from the person's activities at work and outside work. One of the problems is that it is often difficult for an individual to show compelling evidence of his or her leadership ability when carrying out the everyday job. For this reason, it is important to find out what people have done with their lives so far, outside work. The fact that somebody has led a youth club at some time, helped to organise social functions, or even done some political canvassing (the party is irrelevant) is evidence that that person has the ability and the urge to influence others. Often this is more important than the fact that an employee has above-average technical skill.

At the same time, group leaders need to have enough

technical knowledge to protect them from having the wool pulled over their eyes. In general, however, an individual who is acceptable as a leader will always be supported by the group, while an unacceptable 'expert' may well be destroyed.

'Leadership is the gift of the group'

To illustrate this controversial argument on being acceptable or not acceptable, a case can be quoted. An extremely good and hard working estimator was promoted to section leader in the same department due to his boss becoming engineering manager. Had this person been observed carefully, it would have been seen that he was very much a loner and never took part in any of the section's social activities. He was quiet, not very creative but very efficient. When told of his promotion, he was asked if there were any courses he would like to attend. He asked for one on finance and statistics, both subjects very useful to an estimator. He had received no management training throughout his career.

The net result was that, in a very short time, the new supervisor had tried to change everyone to his mode of operation and was most adamant about it. He was also selecting, and doing himself, certain projects that he enjoyed. The work-group gradually withdrew co-operation and the section work rate fell. Within a month, the entire staff had applied for transfers. At the stage when the staff were talking about 'either he goes or we do' an awakened manager saved the situation—just.

A job cropped up abroad to which the new supervisor was sent. Meanwhile, the right number two was selected, given a short course, and took over estimating. On return to home base, the supervisor was counselled and attended an in-depth management course. Somewhere along the line, realisation dawned, because he is now a very effective manager within the same organisation and, in fact, remembers well what acceptability means. Quite often, unfortunately, the traits causing this problem are too firmly fixed to be easily changed. So care must be taken with selection.

When selecting supervisors, study all the information on their work experience, acceptability, room for growth, etc., then ask the question: what have they done to enhance their own prospects? Have they been attending evening classes, carried out home study, or indeed made any effort to make them a better 'buy' as a future supervisor?

Psychological testing

The last few years have seen a dramatic increase in the use of psychological or psychometric tests for the selection of supervisors. Far from being designed to delve into the psyche and expose obscure personality defects, proven psychometric tests offer a means of assessing a candidate's characteristics in a standardised, objective and, it is claimed, more reliable and more valid way than conventional interviews. That is not to say that tests could or should replace interviews; they are complementary techniques which, when used properly, aid the selection process.

According to the British Psychological Society's definition, tests cover a wide variety of aspects, including: intelligence; ability; aptitude; language development and functions; perception; personality; temperament and disposition; interests; habits; values; and preferences. Given such breadth, it is hardly surprising that a bewildering array of tests are available—more than 600 are in use in the UK.

They have four main uses:

1 to help shortlisting, particularly when large numbers of applicants are involved
2 as part of a standard selection procedure (internally or externally)
3 as part of a concentrated assessment of the final few
4 to help existing employees to make career development decisions.

Many companies use the Assessment Centre approach, where a group of potential supervisors are assessed by a variety of techniques over a day or two. Aptitude tests, personality assessments, interviews and group exercises may be included. Several assessors usually rate a group of candidates.

Provided they are carefully chosen and used expertly, tests have a very valid role to play in selection procedures.

4

PREPARING FOR
SUPERVISION

It seems inconceivable that we would put an untrained operator in control of expensive equipment. Yet, often, supervisors are thrust into a situation of producing results through people, with little or no preparation for handling that element of their job.

In learning to swim, it would be considered doubtful if the method used was to throw people in the deep end of a pool without instruction on the very basic rudiments of keeping their heads above water. There are, of course, advocates of the 'deep end' technique of training supervisors, but this is incompatible with the professionalism exhibited in most other aspects of business.

Many people are promoted due to what is known as situational leadership. This is based on the assumption that the person with the most 'know-how' in technical terms is the best candidaate for being boss. Just how many people were promoted from tool-maker to tool room foreman because they happened to be the best tool-maker, or to sales manager because they were the best salesman, nobody knows. The quotation 'authority flows from the one who knows' perhaps sums it up best.

Most supervisors will be familiar with routine and have technical experience, but in dealing with people they are perhaps at their biggest disadvantage. In many cases, it is assumed that they would acquire this ability through some undefined, almost mystical process, and it is to their credit that many of them manage not only to survive but progress to greater things.

In today's environment of requiring work-group leaders to

use leadership skills even more, this method is perhaps anachronistic, to say the least.

To refer to the swimming analogy again, it is often stated that the younger one starts, the easier it is, but many people do not learn to swim until they are adults. The same is certainly true of supervisors. Many do not have the opportunity to take on the responsibility of being a work-group leader until well into their adult life, when personality, etc., is usually well and truly developed. Therefore, 'deep ending' them may well have the effect of putting them off supervising for ever.

Perhaps in both cases, the wisdom of gradual immersion is one that would meet both needs, but particularly in preparation for supervision.

Gradual preparation

Listed are some examples of providing opportunities for gradual immersion. All these examples should be used as an opportunity for real delegation and not some pseudo-exercise, otherwise cynicism, demotivation, etc., will set in.

- Standing in for someone.
- Taking charge of a small section.
- Taking charge of a project.
- Overtime relief.
- Holiday relief.
- Progressive delegation.
- 'The grand tour'.

Standing in

There are many and varied ways in which this can be achieved—sickness, when other people are on courses, secondments, etc. It is important to outline to people who are standing in, the extent of their authority and responsibilities, and to tell all those who will be concerned with them.

Taking charge of a small section

It is worth considering giving a part of a department area over to prospective supervisors to see how they cope. This is particularly feasible if the department tends to be on the large side, e.g. 18 people—give the person responsibility for six people and a specific part of the operation.

Project leading

This method is strongly favoured by many companies as it is 'low risk—high gain' to them. It has the advantage of monitoring potential supervisors in terms of their interaction with people in a leadership position. It also, more often than not, deals with a project that line management gets round to later rather than sooner. There is spin-off in obtaining practice in report writing, fact finding, etc.

Overtime relief

Similar in many ways to standing in, but with a difference. If the trainees are *always* the overtime relief, it may be perceived by them as meaning that that is all they are capable of.

Holiday relief

Similar to standing in and overtime relief, but it would help if the term 'acting in place of' was used, as this would establish quite firmly that the person was the 'head of department' while the incumbent was away.

Progressive delegation

This is where certain responsibilities and authority are given up to a trainee by the supervisor on a gradual basis until the trainee is promoted to take over a specific area. It is essential that this is true delegation and not just turning the trainee into a glorified message carrier. True delegation is not only giving people extra responsibility, but also the relevant amount of authority to enable them to fulfil that responsibility.

'The grand tour'

Sometimes used to describe some of the above, this should not be just 'tagging along' behind the department head. This is very boring to the trainee and an irritant to the boss, as he or she will tend to view the person concerned as a nuisance and 'getting in the way'. This can involve experience in a number of interrelated departments.

One final point on all these methods, and that is that *all* concerned must be notified when a trainee is embarking on the above. Few things can be more demotivating to someone finding their feet in a new role than to be confronted with either indifference or hostility because others concerned had not been informed that the trainee was indeed in charge!

Planned preparation

The next stage in the operation is to have a formal plan. Before and after each 'lesson' it is essential to carry out the basic management functions of:

1 monitor
2 appraise
3 counsel
4 evaluate.

Monitor

Not a licence for breathing down people's necks: it means what it says. A clear definition of responsibility/authority is essential and a sensible system would be regular checks, e.g. each morning/each evening/start of shift, etc. Monitor means to look at results, not inhibit actions.

Appraise

This can be done weekly/monthly/quarterly while monitoring. This will be useful for a fuller appraisal (long-term) either at the end of a 'gradual immersion' period, when annual appraisal is due, or more specifically when considering someone for a full supervisory position.

Counsel

Counselling should be seen as an integral part of a continuous process rather than a 'one-off' at annual appraisal. This would cover such areas as:

- training needs
- possible action(s) by both
- help required
- guidance on studies
- assistance with day release, night classes, etc.

Evaluate

This is so often only done in the narrow confines of the job and ignores or neglects the need in terms of people's development. People need to have their progress evaluated. This is a time for reviewing progress, analysing strengths and weaknesses, looking at possible promotions, or even a change of function, e.g. from production to planning. The golden rule here is *never make promises!* There is no absolute guarantee of future promotion. Broken promises (or what was believed to be a promise) have been the cause of tremendous frustration and disillusionment leading to cynicism and bitterness that is almost impossible to erase.

An important part of 'preparing for supervision' is induction. Almost always associated with new starters, it is not readily apparent that some induction is required even for those 'old hands' if they are embarking on this new era in their working experience.

To meet this new need, a simple induction checklist will suffice. It is desirable that both boss and supervisor-designate have a copy. An example is shown in Appendix 5.

Sponsor

The use of a sponsor is being adopted by a number of organisations. This sponsor is there to help people through a new situation in terms of new geographical knowledge, terminology, customs, etc. Basically a friend in the early days, a sponsor should be someone who has specific responsibility and ability to carry out this role.

5

TRAINING YOUR
SUPERVISORS

The main difference between preparing for supervision and training your supervisors is that the first is concerned with in-company or in-house experience, while the training we are to talk about is concerned with the formal approach off-the-job.

It has been mentioned that, if the prospective supervisor has bothered to attend relevant courses, this should be taken into account. The fact that people have spent their own time and money to better their own ability must be advantageous. The biggest problems encountered, when talking about longer courses, are if people are on shift work, especially if it is a rotating type of shift. These problems can, however, be overcome with the help of good management and flexible training organisations.

Qualifications

The certificate awarded by the National Examinations Board for Supervisory Studies (NEBSS) is one of the main qualifications for supervisors. There are three NEBSS courses: an Introductory Course (30 hours); the Certificate Course (240 hours); and the Diploma Course (an extra 180 hours). Subjects covered relate to organisational and supervisory skills. The candidates also complete a work-related project.

In 1988, there were 410 centres which were authorised to run the courses. Half are training departments of major companies; the balance are further education colleges. There were some 13,000 NEBSS students in 1988, approximately 80 per cent of whom were already in supervisory jobs. The number of candidates is increasing at a rate of 20 per cent per year.

NEBSS have also developed an excellent package of open learning books and tapes. These were originally sponsored by the Training Agency and the series contains 42 titles.

The other qualifications for first line managers are courses accredited by the Institute of Supervisory Management (ISM). The ISM offers a similar range of programmes, from its Introductory Certificate to its Diploma in Management. The latter, whilst a nationally recognised qualification in its own right, also leads to corporate membership of the Institute.

The ISM's Certificate and Diploma do not depend on a formal examination to determine success or failure, but rely on a process of continuous assessment. This involves a series of written assignments during the programme, a project, and an oral presentation—the latter is considered important not only as a means of assessment, but also as a yardstick in the student's progress towards self-confidence and ability.

In-house ISM courses are tailored to specific company needs so that the programme is more work-relevant and has a direct effect on the student's job. Both the Certificate and Diploma courses require 180 hours contact time (or the equivalent in open learning work) and may be completed over two years. In line with the Training Agency's concept of experiential learning, the ISM will recognise proven prior achievement which may reduce the length of these courses.

Whereas experience and ability are essential requirements of any level of management, formal training is also important. There are many approaches, but some form of regular, structured, and preferably participative and practical training should be programmed into all supervisors' schedules.

It is most likely that the training methods used in your organisation combine inside, on-the-job, and off-the-job methods. By sending supervisors to external courses, one can help to broaden horizons, develop self-confidence and make them realise they are not alone in facing the challenges in the job. Because a mixed bag of experience and background is 'round the table', supervisors can gain a different insight into how to operate, and make them test their ideas and views 'away from home'.

6

THE SUPERVISOR AS
A LEADER

Ask any manager above first line level what a good supervisor should be and the chances are he or she will reel off a list of qualities not unlike this:

- resilient
- courageous
- dependable
- forceful
- decisive
- dedicated
- judicious
- understanding
- ambitious
- humorous.

Indeed a similar response would follow should the question: 'What should a leader be?' be asked of any given group of people.

This has been (and still is in many organisations) the method of selecting people for positions of responsibility for as long as anyone can remember. Certainly, our military establishments are littered with quality-like phrases such as integrity, etc.

Action-centred leadership

The problems of selecting people for promotion or a position of leadership by this method became apparent to Dr John Adair, and it is to his work that this chapter is credited, interspersed with current experiences.

It is virtually impossible to arrive at an agreed list of qualities, as first there is usually an argument about the meaning of words. For example, is dependable the same as reliable?

Even supposing agreement was reached on the list of qualities necessary, the next hurdle to be overcome is the one of subjectivity. In deciding upon a prospective candidate by comparing that person against a list of qualities, the selector is being totally subjective. Should more than one person be involved in passing judgement, there is a good chance they will disagree on which qualities the candidate does/does not possess. This is simply because it *is* subjective and is largely one person's *opinion* about another.

Dr Adair's theory, therefore, is based on the very simple premise that if people cannot be trained to *be* something, they can be trained to *do* things. He calls it the functional approach. As a result of his research, which was considerable, a method of training was devised which he called Action-Centred Leadership. This simply means what it states, leadership centred around the action of the leader. Instead of looking at what a leader should be, the concept simply looks at what a leader does.

Adair saw that there are three key areas to be considered, and outlined them as:

- achieve the task
- develop the individual
- build the team.

It is the leader's job to see that these three basic needs are met. This method of developing/improving leadership still applies to new and established supervisors.

Achieve the task

A team with a leader exists because its purpose or task cannot be achieved by one person alone. It is this common purpose which distinguishes the team from a random crowd.

The members of the team feel a strong need to accomplish the task and they need to feel their leader will enable them to do this. They want to feel the leader can plan, organise and control effectively, that the leader knows what is trying to be achieved and that their work is effectively directed towards a relevant goal.

If they do not feel this, and if it becomes evident that they are not achieving this task (e.g. if there are constant shortages of materials), they become demoralised and frustrated. This will happen however well and humanely they are treated by their leader, or however much they like that person.

Develop the individual

Each member has individual needs.

Team members need to: know what is expected of them; feel they are making a significant and worthwhile contribution to the task; receive adequate recognition for this. They need to feel that the job is demanding the best of them; that their abilities are not under-used; that they have responsibility to match their capability; that they are being stretched, challenged, enabled to grow in stature psychologically; that they can look back and think 'a year ago I couldn't do this and now I can!'

They need to feel that they belong to the team; that they are accepted and valued members; that they count. Occasionally, they may need help or counselling over some problem which is new, unfamiliar, and therefore unnerving.

If these needs are not met—and it is the task of the leaders to see that somehow or other they are—then they may withdraw from the group. They may be at work but not working.

Build the team

Any group develops its own personality which is distinct from that of its members. This can become apparent when behaviour expressed as an individual is often totally different to the behaviour expressed as a group. This is something unions understand very well, of course, and supervisors would do well to learn.

A group has the power to set its own standards of behaviour and performance and to impose them even when they are contrary to the interests of individuals and the organisation. It is part of the leader's job to gain acceptance from the group.

The leader must consciously take actions that will result in the group developing loyalty to each other, pride in belonging, a desire to work together as a team, the standards they will accept and once accepted will maintain themselves—in short, morale.

The last point is about using the conflict which will arise in the group to effective ends by not allowing it to become disruptive, nor yet stifling it, but using it for the creativity and ideas it can generate.

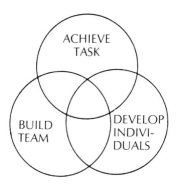

It is no accident that the three circles overlap. The three key areas interact on each other. For example, it is essential for the group to feel they are achieving something in the task before group morale and individual satisfaction can be high. Equally, if the group is torn by internal dissension and jealousies, its performance, as well as individual satisfaction, suffers.

The balanced approach

It is important for the supervisor as the leader to take action to satisfy all three areas. In real life, however, it is not always possible or practicable to give equal attention to all. There will always be instances when leaders have to devote all to the task (to meet a deadline, for example) because the task has priority at that point in time; its need is greatest. This is acceptable, and most thinking people understand when it happens, so long as leaders are aware that they have neglected the other two and, when the first opportunity presents itself, come back and 'recharge' them.

Some supervisors ignore or consistently pay little attention to a particular area of need. There is the familiar 'task orientated' supervisor who tends to ignore people, especially in terms of individuals. They are usually highly efficient, think ahead, give clear instructions and expect them to be obeyed promptly, but are not interested in people as people. Their philosophy tends to be: 'People come to work to do a job; that's what they are paid for, and they don't bring their problems or personal affairs with them! I'm not interested in excuses, just results!'

This sort of supervisor, although highly, even ruthlessly efficient, does get results in the short term but usually fails to obtain the most effective results in the long term. This is often evidenced by poor results getting worse, suspect quality and above-average problems of discipline, etc. If the potential of the individuals was harnessed, better longer-term results would be achieved. This is even more forcibly demonstrated if the 'individual' circle is removed or blacked out in the diagram: it takes a bite from the other two showing that neither the needs of the task are being fully met, nor is the group morale as high as it could be.

Next there are 'people-orientated' supervisors. Their philosophy is: 'If you treat people right they'll work without any pushing.' It is not that they fail to get results but, whenever there is a conflict between demands of the task and the needs of the individual, then it is usually the latter which will gain their support.

This approach is perhaps better illustrated by the repair shop manager who said: 'We don't repair many engines here, but we have a happy shop.' These people usually make a point of, indeed pride themselves on, knowing the personal background of all their people, and follow the progress of their families, their illnesses, their holidays, their children's educational successes and failures, with great interest. They usually attract great loyalty, but there is a vague sense of unease among the group, knowing that they are not being as successful as they could or even should be. Not achieving. The diagram once again demonstrates this: if the task circle is blacked out it can be seen to take a bite out of the team and individual circles. Individuals know they are not being stretched and will turn their energies to other aims which are generally not those of the organisation. It is important for supervisors to be balanced in their approach.

Delegation

It is worth getting supervisors to think about delegation and what they really understand by the true meaning of the word. Delegation is not allocating work as so many supervisors and managers tend to think, but giving people the *right to be wrong*. That is, giving people defined limits, etc. (responsibility/authority), and *letting them get on with it*. The leader then monitors the results, not the actions (*see Delegation*, in this series).

Structure

What is the effect of the organisation structure on the supervisor's leadership?

Frequently, we employ other people to help with task functions, such as helping with technical problems, maintaining quality standards and deciding work priorities. They may handle team functions like arranging holiday cover, implementing safety procedures, and, in particular, communication (*see* Chapter 7). They will commonly deal with individual functions such as selection, grievance, discipline and counselling interviews and decisions, following-up absentees, and induction training.

These people include advisory staff such as training officers, quality inspectors, personnel officers, and safety officers. The more these functions are divided up, the more the team members will be confused about 'who is my leader'.

It is vital to supervisors' effectiveness as leaders that these functions should be their responsibility. Although they may delegate them to others, they retain accountability.

It therefore follows that, in order to fulfil these responsibilities to the full, the supervisor's team should not consist of more than 15 people. As far as possible, too, people should always report to the same boss and not to varying bosses according to shift pattern.

Leadership training

Action-Centred Leadership, a simple but practical method of leadership (management), has been adopted by many companies and thousands of supervisors and managers have received training in it.

In almost all cases, the companies themselves have reported improvements in the managerial behaviour of their supervisors, resulting in better task results, increased team work, and greater satisfaction for individuals.

7

COMMUNICATION

The reactions to the word 'communication' may not be the same from everybody, but there *is* always a reaction and it is usually instant. When carrying out surveys within organisations, it can be almost guaranteed that communication will come out among the top three problem areas. Herzberg lists company policy and administration as the number one dissatisfier on his needs and motivation survey. More recently, some people have translated this as being entirely due to poor communication. That is to say, what percentage of the employees of any organisation really know—let alone understand—the policy and aims of the organisation for which they work? So we find at all levels, in spite of the sheer bulk of communication that goes on, that the effectiveness of this communication is sometimes in doubt. What really is needed is more *effective* communication—not *more* communication. As supervisors have direct contact with the largest part of the workforce, they have one of the most important roles in the communication network.

Supervisors and communication

In as much as supervisors are at the front line of management, the point of production or service, so it is often at this point that trouble can start. Supervisors often complain quite vehemently that their authority has been eroded and their influence taken away.

Let us then look at what has or is happening in the area of communication and how it applies to the supervisor. If there is a query and a meeting called 'upstairs', there often is a shop steward, an operative, and various experts present, plus, of course, the responsible senior managers. Where is the supervisor? Usually working! If there has been a management–union meeting, who tells the workforce of the results? Not the supervisor: he wasn't present!

That is one side of the coin for which the supervisor is not entirely responsible. There is, however, another side. When faced with a query on wages, holidays, sick leave, safety, training, etc., what happens? Not always, but quite often, the supervisor will redirect the employee to some specialist area, i.e. personnel, computer department, wages department, safety officers, training manager, etc. All these items are involved with direct communication, and by not dealing with them or being involved, the supervisors are being stripped, or stripping themselves, of their authority. Indeed it can happen that, by habit, people will go directly to the expert without involving the supervisor at all. Supervisors must be equipped to cope in this area.

This is only part of the complete communication system, but an important and regular part. All that is left for the supervisor as regards personal contact, is to dish out work and discipline, both of which do not necessarily build up good relationships.

Involvement

The effective supervisor must be fully involved at all points of communication to and from the boss and to and from the work-group. To work well, this must be the policy of top management and a matter of procedure. For maximum effectiveness, supervisors should be involved in consultation, decision-taking, and allowed to have a say in negotiations in as much as it may affect their work and their people.

To make this communication function of the supervisor work well, the procedure must be drawn up correctly and adhered to. No one would doubt the unions' right to represent their members' needs, problems and aspirations upwards to management, but they are not management's communication link downwards. Neither is it the 'top person's' job to do this communication, thus bypassing the first line supervisor. There is hardly ever a need to bypass set procedure through the chain of command.

It must be ensured that supervisors are not allowed to short-cut the system through ignorance, pressure of work or, indeed, laziness. They are responsible for getting work done by their people and for their people's well-being. Therefore, they must have available all the information required to answer queries or, if it should be a query they cannot answer, they must know where or who can answer it and find the answer themselves, quickly—not abdicate that responsibility to someone else. If ever employees should be found asking for information of other than their immediate supervisor, they should be asked if they have seen their supervisor first.

A well-worn saying, worth repeating, illustrates this: 'People who communicate—lead.' A simple rule for supervisors for effective communication is:

- *understanding*—(what)
- *acceptance*—(why)
- *action*—(do)
- *check*—(feedback)

No communication has really worked unless people have clearly understood 'what' is required. Following this understanding, an effort must be made to gain acceptance. Resulting from this should arise some action. The wise person will then always build in regular checks to ensure that the required action has taken place as and when needed.

Team briefing

One certain way of re-establishing the supervisor in the chain of command is to install team briefing. This is a well tried and practical drill that ensures all necessary and relevant information is passed from the top to the bottom of an organisation on a regular basis. This information is collated in a manner that can be put across in an interesting and relevant form. At this stage, it is important to anticipate questions that may arise.

Following the accountability chart procedure, managers brief their immediate subordinates in a structured manner. Hence, the briefing day may start with the works manager briefing their supervisor at, say 10 a.m. This briefing should not exceed 30 minutes. Following this meeting, supervisors will brief subordinates—preferably within the hour.

By this method, a very large number of people can be briefed in a very short time, thus stopping any rumour being spread on the grapevine. By communicating on such a regular basis, subordinates start to respond to *their* boss as being the person who tells them the news.

The period between briefings may vary from one organisation to another but must be at regular intervals. One well known and efficient high street store briefs on a weekly basis and gets answers from the feedback the following week. A famous brewery works successfully on a monthly briefing basis, while a successful shipyard finds it effective to brief at six-weekly periods. All, however, keep it regular; all back up the briefing with notes to those who brief to ensure accuracy; and all ensure that queries raised during the feedback session are answered.

This is not the place to delve deeply into team briefing, but suffice to say it is a system which brings supervisors back into the first line of communication and re-establishes their position of authority (*see The manager's responsibility for communication*, in this series, and *Team briefing*, also from The Industrial Society).

8

DEVELOPING AND
MAINTAINING PROGRESS

Recalling the comments about 'deep end' techniques earlier in the book, this can be further developed.

Accepting that it is not a bad idea to teach people the fundamental strokes, once these are mastered, progress can be made towards showing some alternative methods. Once supervisors are through the basics and functioning well, it is in everyone's interests to build on these foundations.

Questions to ask

In order for some supervisors to do their jobs effectively and develop as individuals, they must know the answers to these basic questions.

- What is my job? (Responsibilities/authorities)
- Who is my boss? (Work-group leader)
- What is expected (Standards of performance)
- How am I doing? (Appraisal)
- Where do I go from here? (Evaluate)
- How do I get there? (Counsel)

1 *What is my job?*

In simple terms, outlines to whom and for what people are accountable. How much authority they have to enable them to carry out the job they are being asked to do. Clears up any doubtful areas that might exist about who is to be responsible for certain things. This is particularly important to avoid overlapping between boss and subordinate.

2 *Who is my boss?*

Clears up who it is the supervisor is accountable to for all things, particularly those outlined in (**1**) above.

3 *What is expected?*

A standard of performance is a yardstick for measuring *acceptable* performance. Standards should:

* be realistic not idealistic
* be measurable in some way
* leave room for improvement.

Their purpose is to be able to see in an *objective* way whether or not the job has been carried out to the standard required.

4 *How am I doing?*

Means what it says. It is an opportunity to look at:

* the job as it has been carried out
* what plans can be made for the future.

5 *Where do I go from here?*

An honest *joint* assessment of what is required, in the form of actual plans, from both boss and subordinate to be able to achieve progress.

6 *How do I get there?*

This requires the boss to *guide* the subordinate as to what needs doing to achieve the plans set out. It is essential that the boss does not succumb to the temptation of deciding for the subordinate. This very often *prevents* personal development and growth, rather than promoting it.

By analysing (**4**) and (**5**) a plan of action under (**6**) can be decided on. Decisions regarding action or non-action, methods, areas of development, can be made. Often, the temptation, once supervisors are beginning to show some progress, is to thrust them forward before they are ready (e.g.

having just completed one length of a pool successfully, entering them for a cross-channel swim!). If the person concerned then fails, the Peter Principle of 'being promoted above the level of their competence' is often inappropriately quoted.

In certain cases, it is probably essential that supervisors be allowed to continue in the function they are already in without any additional responsibility, etc. This will at least give them the opportunity to become much more experienced at that stage of their development before moving on.

Considerations for development

It is at this stage that counselling ability on the part of the supervisor's bosses is vital, because the keenness of the supervisors may prevent them from accepting the need to consolidate. The following points should be considered.

- *Span of control.* Is this correct? Could it now be extended? Should it be shortened?
- *Latent ability/skills.* Can they be better employed in another function?
- *Exposure in other functions.* A period in sales. quality control, etc. Builds flexibility and wider understanding. Will help with the question above.
- *Targets.* Setting work-related targets which will provide a challenge and stretch the individual (*see Target setting*, in this series).
- *Projects.* Special areas of investigation, etc.

At appraisal is the time where the above will be discussed and it is important that emphasis is put on the fact that identifying weaknesses is not failure! (*See Appraisal and appraisal interviewing*, in this series.)

II

APPENDICES

APPENDIX 1

THE SUPERVISOR AS A PROFESSIONAL MANAGER

The aims of the Institute of Supervisory Management are summed up in its Motto:

> To encourage and develop the science and practice of supervisory management and to gain recognition of supervisory management, as a profession.

The Institute believes that supervisory management forms part of the total profession of management. The use of the term 'profession' is to affirm that supervision is a calling in the strictest definition: a vocation in respect of which there is a recognised body of knowledge, whose practitioners are under obligation to extend that knowledge and to adhere to accepted standards of conduct and ideals of service.

The essential objectives of the Institute are therefore:

> the promotion and development of the science of supervisory management in industry, trade and commerce, and

> the advancement of education, particularly industrial and commercial education, involving the study of the skills of supervisory management for the benefit of the community in the fields of industry, trade and commerce.

Founded over 40 years ago in the West Midlands, the Institute quickly established itself on a national basis and now enjoys international stature. Members are drawn primarily from industry, commerce and the armed forces, with the civil service, local government and the academic world also well represented. Entry to the professional grades of membership has always been rigorously linked to educational achievement with advancement to the higher grades of membership being dependent upn appropriate professional experience and achievement. Total membership is currently in the order of 15,000 and growing steadily. The Institute seeks to fulfil its objectives by sponsoring professional activity at national level, whilst in many areas of the country, active Regions and Sections organise regular programmes of professional, educational and social activities at local level.

On the educational front, the institute has a long and honourable record of liaison both with companies and colleges. It has always been in the forefront of imaginative, innovative and flexible educational developments without prejudice to standards. Certificate and Diploma courses are available at colleges throughout the country and many 'in-company' training courses are fully accredited for Institute membership.

Recent developments in the field of management education have not passed the Institute by. It was a pioneer of distance learning and is also participating actively in the current 'Management Charter' debate. The Institute is strongly represented on the Council of, and works in close co-operation with, the National Examinations Board for Supervisory Studies. These various educational activities have been reflected of late in the decision of the Council of Management of the Institute having launched a series of national awards:

The ISM Industrial Scholarship, tenable at Durham University.

The ISM Supervisor of the Year Award.

The ISM National Training Award.

Perhaps the best indication of the stature of the Institute and its courses is the educational world, is the fact that it is now possible to proceed via a series of 4 steps, commencing with the ISM Certificate and culminating with a Master of Business Administration degree.

The Institute of Supervisory Management welcomes opportunities to liaise with industry in order to establish the training needs of supervisors, or to negotiate accreditation of company courses.

Please write or telephone G. L. D. Alderson, Director, Institute of Supervisory Management, 22, Bore Street, Lichfield, Staffs WS13 6LP. Tel. (0543) 251346.

APPENDIX 2

SUPERVISING PEOPLE AT WORK

The most important asset that any organisation possesses is its employees. Supervisors, i.e. first line managers, are in a unique position to influence the workforce to give their all to the job.

- **Recognise effort**
  When an employee makes a genuine effort, be sure to show encouragement and appreciation. A pat on the back is often a stronger motivator than a kick in the pants.

- **Team spirit**
  This can be ruined by conflict and argument within a team. Always try to resolve disagreements between individuals at the early stages. Talk to your team, in a group, on a regular basis. Keep them informed of progress and listen to their comments.

- **Consult**
  People will feel more involved, important, and committed if you ask their opinion before taking a decision which affects them. You are also more likely to gain acceptance, even if your decision goes against their advice, providing you explain the reasons.

- **Discipline**
  If you constantly 'turn a blind eye' to breaches of set standards you will soon lose respect (and sometimes control). The team are looking to you to take action against the offender and will become frustrated with your reluctance to talk to the individual. Remember, however, never to reprimand in public.

- **New employees**
  The first few days in a new organisation are important for the new employee. It is also important to you that the new starter settles in quickly and becomes productive. Induction should be tackled in a planned systematic manner by working through a checklist.

- **Training**
  You cannot expect people to work effectively unless they are properly trained. Training is your responsibility. Aim to identify areas that need improvement and arrange training.

Do's and don'ts

Do:

- Give credit where it's due.
- Make sure they get their 'grouses off their chest' by talking to you.
- Stop minor faults developing into major ones by acting early.
- Say what you think—tactfully.
- Let them know how they are doing.
- Take pride in the work of your department—it's contagious.
- Be enthusiastic—even if you don't feel that way.
- Be a good listener—and be available.
- Rotate boring jobs.
- Reprimand only in private.

Don't:

- Be seen to have favourites.
- Ridicule or ignore suggestions.
- Run down management in front of your team.
- Fail to reprimand when a reprimand is deserved.
- Ignore their opinions.
- Withhold information unnecessarily.
- Invent fictitious reasons and excuses to save face.
- Make decisions they should be making.
- Make a subordinate feel a failure.
- Treat mistakes as crimes.

35

APPENDIX 3

EXAMPLE JOB DESCRIPTION
FOR A TYPICAL SUPERVISOR

This is intended to illustrate the type of things that should be looked at. It should be concise and not attempt to cover detail areas which tend to make the job description restrictive.

Job Description Part 1

Salary scale: **Job title:** Supervisor
Code: **Name:**
Unit: Widget assembly

1   Overall purpose of job (objective)
(State primary contribution of the job to the efficient operation of the business.)

To ensure the effective use of resources supplied to reach the agreed production of widgets both quality and quantity. To satisfy needs of customers and suppliers.

2   Position in organisation
Directly responsible to: Production Manager,
                                            Widget production

Directly responsible for (subordinates)   6 assemblers
plus such staff as from time to time may   2 fitters
be assigned to your section: 1 packer
                                            1 clerk

Regular liaison with:
internal—production control, stock ordering, despatch, design office
external—approved suppliers.

3   Personal activities
(List only those activities always carried out by the job holder and never delegated. These will form key areas for standard of performance and targets.)

- Organising and controlling activities of staff for whom responsible.
- Taking part in recruitment and responsible for training.
- Deciding individual work loads to suit production requirements.
- Checking stock availability and production requirements, etc.

4   Authority—specific limits

(State only limits where procedure requires such. Do not limit autonomy and creativity by needless items.)

- Staff. Discipline and training within procedural agreements. Note: direct dismissals can only be recommended, not carried out.
- Buying small items within agreed limits.
- Inform manager if scrap value approaches defined maximum level.
- Arrange overtime to suit requirements up to 10 hours per person per week. Notify manager of all overtime placed.
- Agree standards with staff and inform manager of these standards. Appraise staff and ensure manager has copies of standards and appraisal forms.
- The supervisor is expected to act on his own initiative to attain own standards but should consult with manager in any case where difficulty is encountered.

5   Agreed by .... **Date** ....
Manager's signature

Job Description Part 2

Standards of performance

All standards should be related to activities described in Job Description Part 1. To judge standards, each statement can be prefixed by: the standard of performance has been achieved when . . .

The following rules in preparing standards must be adhered to:

- must be realistic—not idealistic
- must be measurable (quantifiable)
- are continuous and on-going
- must leave room for improvement (in times of urgency)
- must be agreed and understood by boss and subordinate.

Example

Item	Key Area	Standard of performance	Control
1	Communication—internal	In no instances should queries reach manager from initial sources which should have been dealt with by supervisor	Proven occasions of unnecessary queries from the supervisor's/ liaison areas which result from the supervisors' errors (*not to exceed 5*)
2	Communication—external	No unnecessary queries from suppliers within supervisors' areas	Unnecessary queries arising and not put right (*maximum 5 per year*)
3	Finance	To keep within agreed budgets and agreed levels of scrap	Account returns Inspection returns
4	Staff development	All staff to have job descriptions, standards of performance, and be appraised six-monthly	Copies of completed documents
5	Personal development	To carry out personal targets and attend agreed training	Results Report on external course

APPENDIX 4

PROFESSIONAL BODIES AND QUALIFICATIONS

Institute of Supervisory Management
22 Bore Street
Lichfield, staffs
WS13 6LP
05432 51346

ISM Certificate and Diploma in Supervisory Management Studies.
Courses are run in-company and in colleges.

National Examinations Board for Supervisory Studies
76 Portland Place
London W1N 4AA
01-580 3050

Certificate and Diploma in Supervisory Studies.
Courses are run in technical colleges or in-company.

Institute of Administrative Management
40 Chatsworth Parade
Petts Wood
Orpington, Kent
BR5 1RN
0689 75555

Certificate in Administrative Management.
Courses are held at colleges and there are also correspondence courses.

City and Guilds of London Institute
76 Portland Place
London W1N 4AA
01-580 3050

Suggested courses are put on in technical colleges. They lead to assessments and examinations operated by the colleges and City and Guilds jointly as a basis for the award of City and Guilds certificates.

APPENDIX 5

EXAMPLE SELECTION AND INDUCTION TRAINING FROM A LARGE NATIONAL COMPANY

In this company all foremen or supervisors are described as assistant managers thus leaving no doubt as to their status. Although all assistant managers do not necessarily supervise (some are technical specialists) they all follow the same training procedure.

Initially vacancies are advertised across the site. This usually results in some 40 applicants. Only if less than five applications are received would the vacancy be advertised group wide—in practice this has never occurred. The applications are whittled down by a bsic test paper relevant to the type of vacancy and a preliminary interview with two members of the Personnel Department. The top five usually go through but if there are additional, exceptional applicants this number may be increased. Final selection is made by a panel consisting of Chief Production Manager, Department Manager of the department in which the vacancy exists and a member of the Personnel Department. Although this panel selects, the vacancy is not confirmed until satisfactory completion of the training programme. A sample of this programme follows.

Training programme for Tom Smith, Assistant Manager—Process Plant

Week 1

Plant and Process familiarisation

Items to be covered	Location	Date and time	Tutor
Plant and Process:			
Mixing	Tree Top	To be arranged by Tree Top management	Manager or Supervisor
Bottling lines		Wednesday, 2.15 pm	
Laboratory analysis and interpretation of results	Tree Top/ Laboratory		Section leaders, Laboratory
Quality control	Tree Top	To be arranged by Tree Top management	Manager or Supervisor
Quality Control	QT	Friday, 2.15 pm	Mr Brown
Despatch	Tree Top/ Warehouse	Thursday, 9.00–11.30 am	Mr Black
Daily programme	Tree Top	To be arranged by Tree Top management	Manager or Supervisor
Booking product in and out	Tree Top	To be arranged by Tree Top management	Manager or Supervisor
Losses and damaged product			
Stock control, yields and costing	Accounts	Thursday, 2.15 pm	Section leaders, Accounts
Receipt and storage of packing materials	Materials Control	To be arranged by Tree Top management	Mr Green
Purchase of packing materials	Materials Control	Friday, 10.00 am	Mr White

Week 2

Supervisory duties and knowledge

Site tour, noting safety hazards; Inspection of Department, noting all safety hazards	Site and Department	Monday, 9.00 am–lunch	Mr More
Job evaluation system	Management Services	Monday, 2.15 pm	Mr Best
Planning	Planning Department	Tuesday, 2.00–3.30 pm	Mr Young
Certification, absentee returns, sick pay, advances, pension fund, holiday entitlement	Personnel Department	Thursday, 9.00–10.30 am	Mr Old
Labour allocation (key positions/covering/training and training records)	Tree Top	To be arranged by Tree Top management	Manager or Supervisor
Time sheets, absentee recording and overtime rotas	Tree Top	To be arranged by Tree Top management	Manager or Supervisor
Departmental safety, housekeeping, machine guards and safety devices	Tree Top	To be arranged by Tree Top management	Manager or Supervisor

Week 3

Wage structure—industrial relations and grievance procedures	Personnel Department	Monday, 9.30 am	Mr McKenzie
Report writing	Training Centre	Tuesday, 9.00 am	Mr Carter
Safety legislation, company policy and the safety committee		To be arranged	Mr Sykes

Week 3 (continued)

Time sheets and work reports	Wages Department	Thursday, 9.30 am	Miss Jones
Prepration of safety reports	Training Centre	Thursday, 2.15 pm	Mr Carter
Accident reports and procedures	Personnel Department	Wednesday, 10.00 am	Mr Andrews
Discussion of safety report	Training Centre	Friday, am	Mr Campbell/ Mr Carter

Review of progress

During third week to carry out daily allocation of labour and completion of time sheets.

Week 4

Assistant Department Managers, Department A

Week 5

Attend Industrial Society course—Basic Supervision

Week 6

Assist Department Manager, Department B

Weeks 7 and 8

Supervise while assistance available if required.

FURTHER READING

A passion for excellence, by Tom Peters & Nancy Austin. London: Fontana.

Are you managing? By Peter Stemp. London: The Industrial Society.

Delegation, by Andrew Forrest. Notes for Managers. London: The Industrial Society.

Further up the organisation, by Robert Townsend. London: Coronet.

In charge (a supervisor's notebook) by Gordon Rabey. London: Institute of Supervisory Management.

Supervisor's pocket guide, by David Hancox. London: The Industrial Society.

Target setting, by Ian Lawson. Notes for Managers. London: The Industrial Society.

Team briefing, by Janis Grummitt. London: The Industrial Society.

The effective supervisor, by John Adair. London: The Industrial Society.

There is a better way to manage, by Malcolm Bird. Duncan Publishing.